T5-BAF-328

THE
PICTURE COLLECTION
SUBJECT HEADINGS

Parisian adults and children enjoying a variety of pictures in an open-air print stall around 1845. From a color lithograph by Victor Dollet drawn for Goupil, Vibert & Co., Paris.

THE

PICTURE COLLECTION

SUBJECT HEADINGS

By
WILLIAM J. DANE
Art and Music Department
NEWARK PUBLIC LIBRARY
Newark, New Jersey

SIXTH EDITION

THE SHOE STRING PRESS, INC.
1968

Originally published, H. W. Wilson Company, 1910
Second Edition, 1917
Third Edition, 1928
Fourth Edition, 1929
Fifth Edition, 1943

Sixth Edition
©1968, The Shoe String Press, Inc.

SBN: 208 00106 9
Library of Congress Catalog Card Number: 68-54193
Printed in the United States of America

INTRODUCTION

These headings used in the Picture Collection of the Newark
Public Library have evolved over a period of nearly seventy
years and have served to provide visual material to a vast and
changing public with needs ranging from a single illustration of
an everyday subject to groupings of complex visual themes of a
most sophisticated nature. The Collection serves those age
groups ranging from primary school students to retired profes-
sional people and senior citizens.
    The basic philosophy of classification includes following a
scheme whereby small and fragmented topics are grouped under
major headings. This is particularly evident in the areas of
geography and history. For example: Europe-France-Paris-
Eiffel Tower; and Europe-England-History-1714-1917-Hanover-
George III. On the other hand, unique topics are usually
assigned their own headings, such as; Angels; Fortune-tellers;
Grindstones; Mills; Witches. Certain basic headings provide
the classification for great quantities of illustrations. There are
over 100,000 pictures under the two headings, Painters and Portraits, which may be broadly interpreted to include the homes,
family, and documents relating to a particular individual.
    New pictures are selected, classified and processed on a
continual basis and these are selected from picture publishers,
periodicals of all vintage, and from books and other material
which come as gifts or through regular discard procedures in a
large public library system.
    As changes evolve in political geography, science and soci-
ology, new headings are established. Pictures are reclassified
for emerging nations in the world and scientific developments in
automation and space exploration require new headings. Civil
Rights, and Old Age are representative headings reflecting con-
temporary sociological interests.
    As folders of unmounted pictures become bulky, the indivi-
dual pictures are studied with an eye to subdivisions, which are
logical and useful in making it easier to find particular illustrations. Often the pictures themselves provide the best clues to
proper subdivisions. Special collections will necessarily need
to expand headings for topics relating to their field of specializa-
tion. Local history and geography headings may be based on

those in this list under New Jersey; Newark; and United States-
New Jersey. New headings and subdivisions should be readily
established when the need becomes apparent.

The Picture Collection files are open to direct access by the
users and after a minimum of experience, searchers have an
understanding of the basic classification scheme and are thus
able to browse and discover material for themselves. By the
same token, classifiers, filers, and others working for the Collection become familiar with the headings after a minimum of
experience.

Pictures may be mounted or unmounted in the files. The
vast majority are unmounted and are housed in sturdy folders
made from manila sheets, bought in bulk and creased to form a
sort of envelope, suitable for jumbo files. The mounted pictures
on any particular subject are located in front of the folder con-
taining those pictures on the same topic in the folder. All mounts
are uniform board, white, measure 13" x 17-1/2" which is a
proportion based on the golden section; i. e. the short side is ap-
proximately equal to 3/5 of the longer side. Today, as in ancient
times, this proportion has proven aesthetically satisfactory.

Guide cards appear frequently in the files and are designed
to assist the public and the staff to locate specific headings, to
suggest additional headings which expand a topic, or to provide
general information such as definitions, chronologies and re-
lated lists. Guide cards are indicated by strips of bright color
which quickly distinguish them from groups of mounted pictures.

The Picture Collection on which the headings are based, now
includes over one million items and takes in strong supporting
materials of various format including slides, portfolios of plates,
prints, postcards, posters, and picture sets. These collections
are briefly described as the Picture Collection headings are also
used in varying degrees in classifying these visual materials of
varied format. The Slide Collection includes nearly ten thousand
color slides exclusively on art subjects: painting, architecture,
sculpture, graphic and decorative arts and cover the major periods of art history from prehistoric works to the latest contemp-
orary trends such as op and kinetic art. The slides are classified by Dewey and Cutter numbers and are loaned without charge
to adult holders of Newark Library cards.

Over two thousand portfolios of plates are filed adjacent to
the Picture Collection and are accessible to the public through
the regular catalog where they are entered under author, subject
and title cards. The portfolios provide a link between the art
books and the Picture Collection and supplement both. Some of

these portfolios are elaborate and unique publications providing a
wealth of visual material in the areas of ceramics, costume,
furniture, illumination, needlework, rugs, stained glass and textiles in addition to architecture, decoration, painting and sculpture of all periods and cultures. Each portfolio is assigned the
Picture Collection subject heading which most directly relates
to its contents and this heading determines its location on the
shelves.

Prints are maintained in two separate collections; a Circulating Print Collection of 1400 reproductions and a Fine Print
Collection of over 12,000 works of graphic art. The Newark
Library established its circulating print service about sixty years
ago to enable people to borrow reproductions of fine paintings by
major artists and to have the privilege of living with them for an
extended period. The Fine Print Collection is primarily a study
collection of the various media used by graphic artists. Intaglio,
relief, planographic, stencil and experimental techniques are
represented by a wide range of artists and the collection grows
by regular additions. Specialized types of visual material are
processed for inclusion in this collection, for example: music
covers, valentines, historic maps, bank notes, drawings,
Chinese and Japanese prints and books of design, trade cards,
Victorian vignettes, and original works including New Jersey
and Newark iconography. Prints are catalogued with artists,
title, process and subject cards based on the Picture Collection
headings.

The history of poster design is preserved in a collection of
Posters which is housed in oversize files. In the interest of
preservation, posters are stored horizontally as frequent
handling of paper material in this large format results in rips
and tears. They are arranged by topic with separate groupings
for World Wars I & II, travel arranged by country, museums
and gallery announcements, and regular commercial advertising.
The renaissance of poster art including op and psychedelic de-
signs has resulted in an active acquisition policy in this area of
visual record.

Selectivity is of major importance in the Post Card Collection which preserves views of buildings, monuments, landmarks
and scenes which have disappeared or radically changed. Reproductions of paintings and other art works are kept in the post
card file only if the work is not readily available in other visual
collections. Post cards are of a convenient size for use in
opaque projectors and are arranged alphabetically by subject

assigned from the Picture Collection headings. The subject
heading appears on the top right side of the back of each card so
that it can be located while still on file.

Sets of pictures based on curriculum topics are assembled
from the Picture Collection files or obtained directly from picture publishers. These sets are used primarily as direct teaching aids or for classroom or bulletin board displays. Each set
is assigned a subject heading and 20 to 30 pictures are arranged
numerically in the order in which the set should be presented.
Over 600 sets are available to primary and secondary school
teachers with new topics prepared to meet curriculum changes.
Recently organized teaching sets reflect interest in Astronomy,
Community Life, the Early Civilization of the Aztecs, Incas and
Mayans, Negro History Week, Physiology, Simple Machinery,
and the Reconstruction Period of United States History.

It is hoped that this list will serve as a guide to picture
classifiers particularly those establishing new collections.
These headings are the product of many classifiers over a long
period which has seen all of the tremendous changes brought
about during the 20th Century. Millions of pictures have been
located, consulted and borrowed, using these headings and procedures in the Newark Public Library. The headings are an in-
dispensable tool for this Library and one hopes their usefulness
to others will be justification for their publication.

SUBJECT HEADINGS

ABBEYS
> Subdivided by adjective of nationality and further by the name of the abbey.

> See also Cathedrals; Churches; Convents; Monasteries

ADVERTISING
Automobile
Baggage
Banking
Beverages
Books
Candy
Cleaners
Clothing
Container Corporation
Cosmetics
Designers
Direct mail booklets
Food
Historic (by year or decade)
Jewelry
Labels
Layouts
Leather goods
Medicine
Packaging
Perfumes
Textiles
Trade Cards
Travel

AFRICA
> Subdivided by name of country and also by the following:
Desert
Maps
History
History-Manners and customs
People
Resources

AGRICULTURE. See Conservation-Soil; Farm; Fruit growing;
                 Vegetable growing

AIR CONDITIONING. <u>See</u> Heating and ventilating

AIR FORCE
    Subdivided by name of country.

AIRPORTS

AIR RAID SHELTERS

ALMSHOUSES. <u>See</u> Asylums and almshouses

ALUMINUM

AMERICANIZATION. <u>See</u> Flag day; Immigration; Schools-Special;
                          Social settlement; U. S.-History

AMMUNITION
    <u>See also</u> Explosives

AMPHIBIANS
    Caecilians
    Frogs
    Newts
    Salamanders
    Sirens
    Toads

AMUSEMENTS. <u>See</u> Games and amusements

ANGELS
    <u>See also</u> Cherubs; Putti

ANIMALS
    Subdivided by names of animals and the following:
    Collective (for groups of animals of several families)
    In advertising
    In art
    In research
    Maps
    Mythical
    Pet
        <u>See also</u> Animals-cat, dog, mouse, rabbit, etcetera;
                Aquariums; Birds; Fish; Kindness to animals;
                Reptiles-Turtle
    Prehistoric

ANTIQUITIES
    American Indian
    Anglo-Saxon

ANTIQUITIES (cont'd)
  Assyrian (c. 1000-612 B. C.)
  Babylonian (2000-750 B. C.)
  Celtic
  Chaldean (612-538 B. C.)
  Chinese
  Columbian
  Cretan
  East Indian
  Egyptian
  Etruscan
  Greek
  Hittite
  Mannaean
  Mayan
  Mexican
  Minoan
  Persian
  Peruvian
  Phoenician
  Phrygian
  Roman
  Scandinavian
  Scythian
  Sumerian (4000-2000 B. C.)
  Sumerian-Semitic (2500-2000 B. C.)
  Syrian

ANTIQUITIES-NEAR EASTERN.
    See Antiquities-Assyrian (1000-612 B. C.)
              -Babylonian (2000-750 B. C.)
              -Chaldean (612-538 B. C.)
              -Hittite
              -Persian
              -Phoenician
              -Sumerian (4000-2000 B. C.)
              -Sumerian-Semitic (2500-2000 B. C.)
              -Syrian

AQUARIUMS

AQUEDUCTS

ARBOR DAY

ARCHERY. See Sports

ARCHITECTS
  Subdivided by name.

ARCHITECTURAL DETAILS
  Altar
  Arcade
  Arch
  Balcony
  Balustrade
  Capital
  Caryatid
  Ceiling
  Chimney
  Choir stall
  Cloister
  Column
    Composite
    Corinthian
    Doric
    Ionic
    Renaissance
    Roman
    Romanesque
  Confessional
  Cornice
  Court
  Cupboard
  Dome
  Doorway
    American Colonial
  Facade
  Fence
  Fireplace
    American Colonial
    Outdoor
  Floor
  Frieze
  Gargoyle
  Gate
  Lattice
  Marquee
  Moulding
  Pediment
  Pergola
  Pilaster
  Porch
  Pulpit
  Rood Screen
  Roof
  Spire
  Stairway

ARCHITECTURAL DETAILS (cont'd)
  Tower
  Vaulting
  Veranda
  Wall
  Window

ARCHITECTURAL STYLES
  American
  Assyrian
  Baroque and Rococo
  Byzantine
  Chaldean
  Chinese
  Early Christian
  East Indian
  Egyptian
  Gothic
  Greek
  Japanese
  Mohammedan. <u>See</u> Saracenic
  Moorish. <u>See</u> Saracenic
  Renaissance
  Rococo. <u>See</u> Baroque
  Roman
  Romanesque
  Russian
  Saracenic
  Twentieth Century-1900-1919
                   -1920-1929
                   -1930-1939
                   -1940-1949
                   -1950-1959
                   -1960-

ARCHITECTURE-CONTESTS

ARMAMENT
  Armored vehicles
    Half-track
    Tank
  Artillery
    Antiaircraft
    Coastal
    Field
    Historic
    Manufacture
    Naval

ARMAMENT (cont'd)
   Chemical warfare
   Firearms
      Machine Gun
      Pistol
      Rifle
   Hand Weapon
      Bow and arrow
      Club, dagger and knife
      Lance, pike and spear
      Sword
   Missiles and rockets
   Siege

ARMISTICE DAY. See Veterans' Day

ARMOR
   Accessories

ARMORIES

ARMY
   Subdivided by adjective of nationality and:
   United States
      Before 1917
      1917-1920
      1921-1940
      1941-1945
      1946
      Air Corps (Note: after 1947, See Air Force-U. S.)
         Personnel
         Planes
      Parachute and Airborne Troops
      Women
         See also Costume-Military-U. S.; United States-History

ART
   African
   American
      Cigar store Indians
      Colonial
      Figureheads
      Indian
      Restorations
         Cooperstown
         Jamestown
         Shelbourne
         Sturbridge

ART (cont'd)
       Williamsburg
       Winterthur
    Arabian. See Art-Saracenic
    Art Nouveau
    Assyrian (1000-612 B. C.)
    Austrian
    Baroque and Rococo
    Byzantine
    Celtic
    Chaldean (612-538 B. C.)
    Chinese
    Christian
    Collage and Assemblage
    Czechoslovak
    Dadaism
    East Indian
    Egyptian
    English
    Eskimo
    Etruscan
    French
    German
    Gothic
    Greek
    Hittite
    In industry
    Irish
    Italian
    Japanese
    Kinetic Art
    Malay
    Mexican
    Mohammedan. See Art-Saracenic
    Moorish. See Art-Saracenic
    Oceanic
    Op Art
    Persian
    Peruvian
    Pompeian
    Pop Art
    Primitive
    Religious
    Roman
    Romanesque
    Russian
    Saracenic
    Scandinavian

ART (cont'd)
    South American
        Pre-Columbian
        Post-Columbian
    Spanish
    Sumerian (4000-2500 B.C.)
    Swiss
    Syrian
    Turkish. See Art-Saracenic

ART GALLERIES. See Museums

ARTIST. See Occupations-Artists

ASIA
        Subdivided by name of country and further subdivided by city and
        by the following general headings for each separate country:
        History; Manners and customs; Maps; People; Resources.
    Abu Dhabi
    Afghanistan
    Arabia
    Bhutan
    Burma
    Cambodia
    China
    Federated Malay States
    Gaza
    India
    Iran (Persia)
    Iraq
    Israel
    Japan
    Jordan
    Korea
    Kuwait
    Laos
    Lebanon
    Malayasia
    Maps
    Mesopotamia
    Mongolia
    Mountains
    Nepal
    Pakistan
    Palestine
    Qatar
    Rivers

ASIA (cont'd)
    Russia
        Kazaka SSR
        Kirghiz SSR
        Siberia
        Tadzhik SSR
        Turkmen SSR
        Uzbek SSR
    Siam. See Thailand
    Siberia. See Asia-Russia-Siberia
    Sikkim
    Singapore
    Soviet Republic (Asiatic). See Asia-Russia
    Syria
    Thailand
    Tibet
    Turkestan. See Asia-Russia-Turkmen SSR
    Turkey. See Europe-Turkey
    Union of Soviet Socialist Republics. See Asia-Russia or Europe-Russia
    Vietnam
    Yemen

ASIA-INDIA-TAJ MAHAL. See Asia-India-Agra

ASTRONOMERS

ASTRONOMY
    Aurora
    Comet and meteor
    Constellations
    Earth
    Eclipse
    Galaxies
    Moon
    Planets
    *Satellites
    Sun

    *This heading refers to man-made satellites.
    For others. See Astronomy-Planets.

ASYLUMS AND ALMSHOUSES

ATHLETICS. See Games and amusements; Gymnastics; Sports

ATOMIC ENERGY (Includes the atomic bomb)

AUSTRALIA
Subdivided by names of cities and the following:
History
Manners and customs
People
Resources

AUTOMATION

AUTOMOBILE INDUSTRY

AUTUMN

AVIATION. See Air Force; Army-U.S.-Air Corps; Airports; Aviation
industry; Transportation-Air; Transportation-Space

AVIATION INDUSTRY

BAKER. See Occupations-Baker

BANKS
Exterior
Historic
Interior

BARBER. See Occupations-Barber

BASKETRY. See Handicrafts; Indians-Useful arts

BASQUES. See Europe-France-B; Europe-Pyrennes; Europe-Spain-B

BATHS. See Public baths

BATIK. See Design-Batik

BEADWORK
See also Handicrafts; Indians-Useful arts; Needlework

BEE-KEEPING

BELLS

BEVERAGES
Alcoholic
Non-Alcoholic
Processing
See also Advertising-Beverages;Cocoa;Coffee;Hygiene-Food-
Milk;Tea

BIBLE
> Subdivided by names of characters and events.
> > And also Bible-Engravings; Bible-History
> Titles of books of the Bible are not used except Apocrypha,
> Psalms, and Revelations.

BIBLE-CHRIST
> Arranged chronologically. Numbers are used instead of subheads.
1 Annunciation
2 Salutation
3 Nativity, shepherds and magi
4 Presentation in the temple
5 Flight into Egypt and Massacre of the Innocents
6 Childhood of Jesus
7 Christ in the temple
8 Baptism of Jesus
9 Temptation
10 First miracle, marriage at Cana
11 Cleansing of temple
12 Discourse with Nicodemus
13 Woman of Samaria (at well)
14 Healing nobleman's son
15 Preaching in synagogue
16 Miracle, draught of fishes
17 Call of the four; Andrew, James and John, Simon
18 Casting out unclean spirit
19 Healing Simon's wife's mother
20 Healing leper
21 Healing paralytic
22 Call of Matthew
23 Infirm man at pool of Bethesda
24 Disciples plucking grain
25 Healing man with a withered hand
26 Choosing twelve
27 Sermon on Mount
28 Healing centurion's servant
29 Raising widow's son at Nain
30 Anointing at house of Simon by Mary Magdalene
31 Parable of sower
32 Wheat and tares
33 Mustard seed
34 Hidden treasure
35 Last judgment
36 Goodly pearls
37 Net (calling of the 4)
38 Stilling the tempest
39 Gadarene demoniacs
40 Raising Jairus' daughter

BIBLE-CHRIST (cont'd)
    41 Woman touching the hem of His garment
    42 Two blind men and dumb demoniac
    43 Twelve sent on mission
    44 Feeding five thousand
    45 Jesus walking on the water and calling Peter
    46 Discourse on bread of life
    47 Miracles (not otherwise noted)
    48 Syrophoenician woman
    49 Transfiguration
    50 Shekel in fish's mouth
    51 Woman taken in sin
    52 Light of the world
    53 Mission of seventy
    54 Invitation "come unto Me"
    55 Good Samaritan
    56 Visit to Martha and Mary
    57 Bartimeus and man born blind
    58 Good Shepherd
    59 Lord's prayer and discourse on prayer, Knock, etc.
    60 Consider the lilies
    61 Fig tree
    62 Woman healed on Sabbath
    63 Grain of mustard seed
    64 Leaven
    65 Christ weeping over Jerusalem
    66 Parable great supper
    67 Ninety and nine
    68 Woman losing silver pieces
    69 Prodigal son
    70 Unjust steward
    71 Lazarus and rich man
    72 Raising of Lazarus
    73 Healing ten lepers
    74 Importunate widow
    75 Pharisees and publican
    76 Christ blessing children
    77 Rich young ruler
    78 Laborers in vineyard
    79 Claims of John and James for high places
    80 Blind men near Jericho
    81 Zacchaeus
    82 Parable of pounds
    83 Anointing of Christ by Mary
    84 Triumphal entry
    85 Cursing fig tree
    86 Parables (not otherwise noted)
    87 Vineyard (two sons)

BIBLE-CHRIST (cont'd)
  88 Husbandmen
  89 Marriage guest
  90 Tribute money
  91 Widow's mite
  92 Prophecy concerning Jerusalem
  93 Ten virgins
  94 Talents
  95 Judas, conspiracy and repentance
  96 Last supper and washing disciples' feet
  97 Gethsemane and arrest
  98 Trials, flagellation, Peter's denial
  99 Crucifixion and burial
  100 Resurrection
  101 Appearance after resurrection
  102 Ascension
  103 Portraits of the Christ

BIOLOGY
  Botany
  Zoology
    Amoebae and paramecia
    Cells
    Evolution
    Genetics
    Hydra
    Reproduction
      See also Amphibians; Animals; Birds; Physiology; Races;
        Reptiles

BIRDS
    Subdivided by names of birds and the following
  Cages
  Collective
  Eggs
  Flying
  Houses
  Migration
  Nests
  Prehistoric

BLACKSMITH. See Occupations-Blacksmith

BLIND

BOATS. See Navy; Transportation-Water

BOAT-HOUSES

BOOK COVERS
    Children's books

BOOK-END PAPERS
    Marbleized
    Modern
    Old fashioned

BOOK-ILLUSTRATION-HISTORIC

BOOKBINDING
    English
    French
    German
    Italian
    Modern
    Processes

BOOKKEEPER. See Occupations-Bookkeeper

BOOKPLATES

BOOKS-PEOPLE READING
    (Includes Steinweg's picture of the Bookworm of Leary's Book
    Store in Philadelphia.)

BOY SCOUTS

BRICKLAYER. See Occupations-Bricklayer

BRICKWORK
    See also Clay products-Brick; Houses-Exterior-Brick

BRIDGE-BUILDING

BRIDGES
    American
    American-Covered

BRIDGES-NATURAL. See Forms of land and water-Natural bridges

BROTHERHOOD

BROWNIES AND GOBLINS
    See also Fairies

BUILDING CONSTRUCTION

BULLFIGHTING. See Games and amusements-Bullfighting

BUSINESS BUILDINGS

BUSINESS MACHINES
    See also Typewriters

BUTCHER. See Occupations-Butcher

BUTTONS

CABINET MAKING

CABLES. See Communication-Telegraph

CACAO
    Products

CAFES. See Restaurants and Cafes

CALENDARS

CAMEOS

CAMOUFLAGE

CAMPHOR

CAMPING

CANADA
        Subdivided by provinces, territories and additional headings as
        listed below:
    Alberta
    British Columbia
    Lakes and rivers
    Manitoba
    Mountains
    National Parks
    New Brunswick
    Newfoundland
        Labrador
    Northwest Territories
    Nova Scotia
    Ontario
        Niagara Falls
        Ottawa
        Toronto
    Prince Edward Island

CANADA (cont'd)
   Quebec
      Montreal
   Saint Lawrence Seaway
   Saskatchewan
   Yukon
   History
CANADA-Manners and customs
      -Maps
      -People
      -Resources

CANALS
   Subdivided by names of canals.

CANDLES. See Lighting

CARICATURES
   Beerbohm
   Color
   Drama and music
   Foreign
      English
      French
      Latin American
   Judge
   Life
   New Yorker
   Personalities-A-Z
   Politics-Foreign
   Politics-United States
   Public Opinion
   Puck
   Uncle Sam
   Vanity Fair

CARPENTER. See Occupations-Carpenter

CARTOONISTS
   Subdivided by the name of the cartoonist.

CARTOONS
   American Monthly Review of Reviews
   Art
   Harper's Weekly
   Music
   Political
   War

CARVING
    Ivory
    Soap
    Stone
    Wood

CASTLES
    Subdivided by adjective of nationality and further by names of
    castles.

CATHEDRALS
    Subdivided by adjective of nationality and further by names of
    cathedrals.

CAVE DWELLERS. See Habitations-Cave; Races-Prehistoric

CELEBRATIONS. See Ceremonies; Expositions; Fairs; Festivals;
                  Pageants; and names of holidays

CEMENT

CEMETERIES
    See also Crematories; Tombs; Tombstones

CENTRAL AMERICA
    Subdivided by name of republic and colony of British Honduras.
    British Honduras
    Costa Rica
    Guatemala
    Honduras
    Nicaragua
    Panama
    Salvador

CERAMICS
    African. See Ceramics-Primitive
    American
    American Indian
    American-Colonial
    Arabian. See Ceramics-Saracenic
    Austrian
    Belgian
    Celtic
    Chinese
    Czechoslovak
    Danish

CERAMICS (cont'd)
  Design
    Bowl
    Cup
    Plate
    Tableware
    Tea service
    Vase
  Dutch
  East Indian
  Egyptian
  English
    Bow
    Bristol
    Chelsea
    Coalport
    Crown Derby
    Delft
    Elton
    Leeds
    Liverpool
    Lowestoff
    Lustreware
    Minton
    Royal Doulton
    Spode
    Staffordshire
    Wedgewood
    Worchester
  Figure
  French
  German
  Glazes
  Greek
  Hispano-Moresque
  Hungarian
  Italian
  Japanese
  Manufacture
  Mexican
  Moorish. See Ceramics-Hispano-Moresque and Ceramics-Saracenic
  Persian
  Peruvian
  Primitive
  Russian
  Saracenic
  Spanish. See Ceramics-Hispano-Moresque
  Swedish
  Swiss

CEREMONIES

CHARTS. See Drawing-Graph

CHEMISTRY
  Historic
  Industrial

CHERUBS

CHICLE

CHILD LABOR

CHILDREN
  As artist
  Foreign (by nationality)
  In art
  Indoor activities
  Outdoor activities
    Autumn
    Spring
    Summer
    Winter

CHINA. See Ceramics

CHINA PAINTING. See Ceramics-Design; Design-Flower

CHIVALRY. See Middle Ages

CHOCOLATE. See Advertising-Candy; Cacao-Products; Food-Candy

CHOIRS

CHRISTMAS
  Cards
  Decoration
  Design
  Foreign lands
  Gifts
  Historic
    American
    English
  In art
  Music
  Religious

CHRISTMAS (cont'd)
   Santa Claus
   Trees

CHURCH
   Customs
   Decoration
   Furniture
   Plans
   Vestments

CHURCHES
   Subdivided by adjective of nationality and also:
   Churches-United States (by State)

CIDER. See Beverages

CIGAR STORE INDIANS. See Art-American

CIRCUS
   Animals
   History
   Parades
   Performers
     Acrobat
     Clown

CITY HALLS
   Subdivided by adjective of nationality.

CITY PLANNING
   Bird's-eye Views
   Historic
   Maps and squares
   Playgrounds
   Refuse disposal
   Slums
   Urban renewal
   Zoning

CITYSCAPES
   See also City planning; Rendering-Cityscapes

CIVIL RIGHTS

CIVILIZATIONS
   Early-Celtic
     -Minoan
     -Mycenaean
     -Phoenician

CLAY PRODUCTS
    Brick
    Cement
    Hollow tile
    Terra Cotta

CLIFF DWELLERS. See Habitations-Cliff; Indians; Races-Prehistoric

CLIMATE. See Weather

CLOCKS AND WATCHES
    American
    English
    French
    German
    Historic
    Hour Glass
    Manufacture
    Sun Dial
    Swiss

CLOUDS

CLUB HOUSES

COAL. See Mining

COAST GUARD

COAT OF ARMS
    Subdivided by names.

COBBLER. See Occupations-Cobbler

COCOA. See Cacao-Products

COFFEE

COINS
    Ancient
    English
    Mint

COLLEGE LIFE

COLLEGES
    Subdivided by adjective of nationality, also by United States,
    and further by names of colleges.

COLOR CHARTS

COLOR STUDIES

COMMUNICATION
    Newspaper
    Phonograph
    Pigeon
    Postal Service
    Radar
    Radio
    Radio-Programs
    Space
    Telegraph
    Telephone
        Booths and coin phones
        Equipment
        Historic
        Invention of
        Military
        Operators
        Phones
        Switchboards
        Uses of
    Television
    Town Crier

CONCRETE

CONFERENCES (By dates)

CONSERVATION
    Soil
    Wild life. See Fish; Forestry
        See also Pollution

CONVENTS

COOKING. See Home Economics-Cooking

COPPER. See Mining

CORAL

CORK

CORN

COSMETICS (by date)

COSTUME
> Before 1825, fashion plates classified by the following headings
> with national costume also identified by century; i.e., Costume-
> Italian-16th Century. After 1825, fashion plates became inter-
> national in style and are classified by year with added headings
> for Children and Men; i.e., Costume-1864-Children.

Academic
Accessories
> Fan
> Hat
> Headdress & hairstyles
> Jewelry
> Shoes
> Ties

African
Albanian
American Colonial
> Subdivided by twenty year periods from 1620 to 1800; then 1800
> to 1825.

American Indian
Arabian
Assyrian. See Chaldean
Austrian
Bakst. See Costume-Stage; Illustrators-Bakst
Belgian
Biblical
Bulgarian
Byzantine
Central American
Chaldean
Chinese
Clown
College. See Costume-Academic
Czechoslovakian
Danish
Design. See Drawing-Fashion
Dutch
East Indian
Ecclesiastical-Church
Egyptian-Ancient
             -Modern
English
Fancy
Flemish
French-Regional (indicate name of region)

COSTUME (cont'd)
   German
   Greek-Ancient
       -Modern
   Gypsy
   Hungarian
   Irish
   Italian
   Japanese
   Javanese
   Judge
   Lebanese
   Medical
   Medieval
   Mexican
   Military
      English
      French
      German
      Greek
      Italian
      Scotch
      Spanish
      Swiss
      United States (by date)
         See also Armor; Army
   Naval
   Norwegian
   Page
   Persian
   Polish
   Portuguese
   Renaissance
   Roman
   Roumanian
   Russian
   Scotch
   Siberian. See Costume-Russian
   South American
   Space
   Spanish
   Sport
   Stage
   Swedish
   Swiss
   Syrian
   Turkish
   Ukrainian

COSTUME (cont'd)
  Wedding
  Welsh
  West Indian
  Yugoslavian

COTTON

COURT HOUSES

COURTS, LAW
  English

COWBOYS. See United States-Western life

CREMATORIES

CRIME AND CRIMINOLOGY
  Adult
  Juvenile

CROSSES

CROWNS

CRUSADES

CURRENCY
    See also Coins

CUSTOMS HOUSES

CYCLONES. See Storms

DAIRIES

DAMS

DANCERS
    Subdivided by names of dancers

DANCES
  Ballet
  Ballroom
  National
  Oriental

DECORATION. See Architectural Details; Architectural Styles;
Carving; Christmas Decorations; Design; Draw-
ing; Furniture; Houses-Interior; Illumination;
Jewelry; Lettering; Metalwork; Needlework;
Painting; Rugs; Sculpture; Stained glass; Stencils;
Table Decoration; Tapestries

DECORATION DAY

DENTISTRY
    See also Hygiene-Care of teeth; Occupations-Dentist

DESIGN
    American Indian
    Animal
    Arabian
    Art Nouveau
    Baroque
    Batik
    Bird
    Block printing
    Boat
    Border
    Byzantine
    Cards
    Cartouche
    Ceiling
    Celtic
    Chaldean
    Chinese
    Christmas. See Christmas-Design
    Circle
    Coptic
    Corner
    Czechoslovak
    Development
    Dragon
    Dutch
    East Indian
    Egyptian
    Etruscan
    Figure
    Flat. See Design-Surface
    Flower
        Subdivided by names of flowers.
    Flower (Conventionalized)
    French
    Frieze

DESIGN (cont'd)
   Fruit
   Geometric
   German
   Gothic
   Greek
   Hungarian
   Industrial
   Insect
   Italian
   Japanese
   Japanese-Shibui
   Javanese
   Leaf
   Medallion
   Medieval
   Mexican
   Panel
   Panel-color
   Pennsylvania German
   Persian
   Peruvian
   Phonograph record covers
   Polish
   Pompeian
   Primitive
   Psychedelic
   Renaissance
   Rococo
   Roman
   Romanesque
   Rosette
   Russian
   Saracenic
   Scandinavian
   Scroll
   Sea Life
   Spanish
   Square
   Stencils. _See_ Stencils
   Sun
   Surface
   Swiss
   Textiles
      Japanese
      Period
      Scandinavian
   Tibetan

DESIGN (cont'd)
　Tree
　Turkish
　Vignette
　Wall
　Wallpaper
　　Historic
　　Samples
　　Scenic
　Wreath

DESIGNERS
　Subdivided by name of designer.

DEVILS

DISEASES
　Subdivided by name of disease.
　　See also　Medicine; Surgery; X-ray

DIVING
　Includes deep-sea diving, aqualung, etc.
　　See also　Sports-Diving

DOCKS.　See Wharves and docks

DOLLS.　See Toys and dolls

DOMESTIC SCIENCE.　See　Food; Home Economics

DRAPERIES

DRAWING
　Animal
　Architectural
　　See also　Rendering-Architectural
　Bird
　Blackboard
　Brush
　Chalk
　Charcoal
　Crayon
　Fashion
　Figure
　Figure-Draped
　Fish
　Flower

DRAWING (cont'd)
   Food
   Graph
   Hand
   Head
   Insect
   Pastel. See Drawing-Chalk
   Pen and Ink
   Pencil
   Perspective
   Trees

DRAWINGS
    Subdivided by names of artists.

DREDGES

DUELING

DWARFS. See Brownies and Goblins

DYEING

EARTHQUAKES

EASTER

ECONOMICS
    See also Banks; Coins; Currency; U. S. -N. Y. C. -Stock Exchange

ELECTRICAL APPLIANCES

ELECTRICITY

ELECTRONICS

ELEVATORS

EMBLEMS
   American

EMBROIDERY. See Needlework

ENAMELS

ENGINEER. See Occupations-Engineer

ENGINEERING. See Bridge building; Building construction; Occupa-
             tions-Engineer

ENGINES. <u>See</u> Machinery

ENGRAVERS
  Subdivided by names of engravers.

ENGRAVING PROCESSES
  Copper
  Line
  Linoleum
  Mezzotint
  Steel
  Stipple
  Wood
  Wood-Color
  Wood-Early
  Wood-19th Century
  Wood-20th Century

ETCHERS
  Subdivided by name of etcher.

ETCHING PROCESSES
  Subdivided by name of process:
  Aquatint
  Drypoint

EUROPE
  Subdivided by name of country and further subdivided by city and
  by the following general headings for each separate country:
  Government; History; Manners and customs; Maps; People;
  Resources.
  Albania
  Alps
  Andorra
  Austria
  Belgium
  Bulgaria
  Czechoslovakia
  Denmark
  England
      Subdivided by name of city and county and by the following:
  Channel Islands
  Isle of Man
  Isle of Wight
  Lakes Region

EUROPE
  England (cont'd)
    London
      Bird's-eye views
      Bridges
      Buckingham Palace
      Buildings
      Churches
      Dore's illustrations
      Guard
      Historic
      Houses of Parliament
      Maps
      Monuments
      Parks
      Piccadilly Circus
      River scenes
      Street scenes
      Tower of London
      Trafalgar Square
    Rivers
    Rural
  England-Government
    Coronation
  England-History
    Subdivided by major period, dynasty, monarch and also by
    century:
    2500 B. C. -55 B. C. -Prehistoric
    55 B. C. -410 A. D. -Roman
    449-1066-Saxon and Danish
      Alfred the Great
      Sweyn
      Canute
      Edward the Confessor
      Harold
    1066-1154-Norman
      William I
      William Rufus
      Henry I
      Stephen
    1154-1399-Plantagenet
      Henry II
      Richard I
      John
      Henry III
      Edward I
      Edward II

EUROPE
   England-History (cont'd)
       Edward III
       Richard II
      1399-1485-Lancaster-York
       Henry IV
       Henry V
       Henry VI
       Edward IV
       Edward V
       Richard III
      1485-1603-Tudor
       Henry VII
       Henry VIII
       Edward VI
       Mary
       Elizabeth
      1603-1714-Stuart
       James I
       Charles I
      1649-1660-Commonwealth
       Cromwell
      1660-1714-Stuart
       Charles II
       William and Mary
       Anne
      1714-1917-Hanover
       George I
       George II
       George III
       George IV
       William IV
       Victoria
       Edward VII
      1917-Windsor
       George V
      1914-1918-European War
      1917-Windsor
       Edward VIII
       George VI
       Elizabeth II
   Esthonia
   Finland
   France
      Subdivided by province or city and the following:
   Alps
   Engravings

EUROPE
  France (cont'd)
    Maps
    Paris
      Arch of Triumph
      Bird's-eye views
      Bridges
      Buildings
      Churches
      Eiffel Tower
      Historic
      Maps
      Monuments
      Museums
      Opera House
      Palaces
      People
      Place de la Concorde
      Quais
      Street Scenes
      Streets
    Rivers
    Rural
  France-History
    597-58 B. C.-Early
    58 B. C.-481 A. D.-Roman
    481-752-Merovingian
      Clovis
      Dagobert
      Charles Martel-Battle of Tours
    752-987-Carolingian
      Pepin
      Charlemagne
    987-1328-Capet
      Hugh Capet
      Robert
      Henry I
      Philip I
      Louis VI
      Louis VII
      Philip Augustus
      Louis VIII
      Louis IX
      Philip III
      Philip the Fair
      Louis X
      Philip V
      Charles the Fair

EUROPE
  France-History (cont'd)
    1328-1589-Valois
      Philip VI
      John the Good
      Charles V
      Charles VI
      Charles VII
      Joan of Arc
      Louis XI
      Charles VIII
      Louis XII
      Francis I
      Henry II (married Catherine de Medici)
      Francis II)
      Charles IX) - sons of Henry II & Catherine
      Henry III
    1589-1789-Bourbon
      Henry IV
      Louis XIII
      Louis XIV
      Louis XV
      Louis XVI
    1789-1792-Revolution
    1792-1795-First Republic
    1795-1799-Directory
    1799-1804-Consulate
    1804-1814-First Empire
    1814-1848-Restoration
      Louis XVIII
      Charles X
      Louis Philippe
    1848-1852-Second Republic
    1852-1870-Second Empire
    1871-1946-Third Republic
      See also World War 1939-1945. Europe
    1914-1918-European War
    1946-1958-Fourth Republic
    1958-Fifth Republic
    Manners and Customs
  France-Manners and Customs
      -People
      -Resources
  Germany
      Subdivided by city or province, and the following:
    Black Forest
    Rivers

EUROPE
  Germany-History
    600 B. C. -12 B. C. -Early
    12 B. C. -16 A. D. -Roman
    16-481-Wandering of the Nations
    481-911-Frankish
      Charlemagne
      Lothaire I
      Charles the Bald
      Charles the Fat
      Arnulf
      Louis IV
    911-1138-Saxon and Franconian
      Conrad I
      Henry I
      Otho I
      Otho II
      Otho III
      Henry II
      Conrad II
      Henry III
      Henry IV
      Henry V
      Lothaire II
    1138-1271-Hohenstaufen or Swabian
      Conrad III
      Frederick I
      Henry VI
      Philip
      Otho IV
      Frederick II
      Conrad IV
      William of Holland
      Richard of Cornwall
    1271-1347-Hapsburg
      Rudolf I
      Adolf
      Albert I
      Henry VII
      Ludovic V
    1347-1437-Luxemburg-Bohemian
      Charles IV
      Wenceslas
      Robert
      Sigismund

EUROPE
  Germany-History (cont'd)
    1437-1519-Hapsburg
      Albert II
      Frederick III
      Maximilian I
    1553-1618-Hapsburg
      Ferdinand I
      Maximilian II
      Rudolph II
      Matthias
    1618-1648-30 Years War (Hapsburg)
      Ferdinand II
      Ferdinand III
    1648-1871-Hapsburg
      Leopold I
      Joseph I
      Charles VI
      Frederick William I
      Frederick the Great (Prussia - 1740-1786)
      Frederick William II
      Frederick William III
      Frederick William IV
      Francis I
      Joseph II
      Leopold II
      Francis II
      Ferdinand I
      Francis Joseph I
    1871-1918-Hohenzollern
      William I
      Frederick III
      William II
    1914-1918-European War
    1918-1933-Republic
    1933-1945-Third Reich
    1945
    Manners and Customs
  Germany-Manners and Customs
      -Maps
      -People
      -Resources
  Gibraltar
  Greece
    Subdivided by city.
  Greece-History
    Prehistoric-776 B. C.
    776-500 B. C. -Early

EUROPE
    Greece-History (cont'd)
        500-479 B. C. - Persian Wars
        479-359 B. C. - Period of Independence
        359-229 B. C. - Union with Orient
        229-146 B. C. - Union with Occident
        by date
        Manners and Customs
    Holland
    Hungary
    Iceland
    Ireland
        Giant's Causeway
        Killarney
    Italy
            Subdivided by city and the following:
        Alps
        Engravings
        Lakes
        Rome
            Appian Way
            Arches
            Baths
            Bird's-eye views
            Buildings-Capitol
                Castle Sant Angelo
                Pantheon
                Temples. See also Temples-Roman
            Churches
            Colosseum
            Forums
            Fountains
            Monuments
            Vatican
        Venice
            Bridge of Sighs
            Bridges
            Campanile
            Canals
            Doge's Palace
            Etchings and drawings
            General views-Color
            Gondolas
            Historic
            Lido
            Manners and Customs
            Maps

EUROPE
  Italy-Venice (cont'd)
      Palaces
      Piazzeta
      Rialto Bridge
      St. Mark's
      Santa Maria della Salute
      Statues
  Italy-History
    476-1799
    1800-1899
    1900-1946
    1947-
    Manners and Customs
  Jugo-slavia. See Yugoslavia
  Latvia
  Liechtenstein
  Lithuania
  Luxemburg
  Maps
  Monaco
  Montenegro. See Yugoslavia
  Norway
  Poland
  Portugal
  Pyrenees
  Rivers
  Roumania
  Russia
  Russia-History
    to 1688
    1689-1800
    1801-1900
    1904-1905-Russo-Japanese War
    1901-1917
    1917-1923-Revolution and reorganization
    1923-U.S.S.R.
  San Marino
  Scotland
  Spain
    See also Europe-Pyrenees
  Spain-History
    to 1930
    1930-
  Sweden
  Switzerland
    Alps

EUROPE
    Turkey
    Union of Socialist Soviet Republics. See Europe-Russia
    Wales
    Yugoslavia

EXPLORERS
        Subdivided by name.
    Vikings

EXPLOSIVES

EXPOSITIONS
    Alaska-Yukon-1909
    Barcelona-1929
    Brussels-1910
    Brussels-1958
    California-Pacific-1935
    Canada-Quebec. See Quebec-1908
    Centennial-1876
    Chicago-1933-1934
    Columbian-1893
    Great Lakes-1936
    Jamestown-1907
    Lewis and Clark-1905
    Louisiana Purchase-1904
    Milan-1906
    Montreal-1967
    New York-1939
    New York-1964
    Pan American-1901
    Panama Pacific-1915
    Paris-1878
        -1879-1889
        -1900
        -1925
        -1931
        -1937
    Philadelphia-1926
    Quebec-1908
    Seattle World's Fair-1962
    Tokyo-1922
    Turin-1911

FACTORIES
    Exterior
    Interior

FAIRIES
    See also Brownies and Goblins

FAIRS

FAMILY
    Brother and sister
    Father
    Grandparents
    Groups
    In art
    Mother

FAMILY TREES. See Art-American; Printing-History

FANS. See Costume-Accessories

FARM
    Activities
    Animals
        Cattle
        Collective
        Horse
        Pig
        Poultry
        Sheep
    Buildings
    Machinery
    Products

FASHION INDUSTRY

FESTIVALS

FIBERS

FILMS. See Moving pictures

FIRE

FIRE DEPARTMENTS

FIRE PREVENTION

FIREMEN. See Occupations-Fireman

FIREWORKS

FIRST AID

FISH
      Subdivided by name of fish and the following:
      Hatcheries
      Maps
          See also Sea life; Shellfish

FISHING
      See also Sports-Fishing

FLAG DAY

FLAGS
      Subdivided by nation and the following:
      Collective
      Collective-Historic
      Great Britain
      Marine (Includes the international signal code)
      United States
         Historic
         State

FLAX. See Linen

FLOATS

FLOODS AND FLOOD CONTROL

FLOWER ARRANGEMENT

FLOWER STUDIES

FLOWERS
      Subdivided by names of flowers and the following:
      State
      Wild

FOOD
      Bakery
      Breakfast
      Candy
      Dairy
      Dessert
      Dinner and Supper
      Fish
      Fruit
         See also Fruit; Fruit growing

FOOD (cont'd)
    Meat
        See also Meat
    National
    Preservation
    Salad
    Soup
    Vegetables
        See also Vegetables; Vegetable growing

FORESTRY

FORMS OF LAND AND WATER
    Bay
    Brook
    Canyon
    Cape
    Cave
    Cliff
    Desert
    Geyser
    Glacier
    Harbor
    Island
    Isthmus
    Lake
    Marsh
    Mountain
    Natural Bridges
    Ocean
        See also Oceanography
    Peninsula
    Plain
    Plateau
    Pond
    Promontory
    Rapids
    River
    Strait
    Valley
    Volcano
    Volcano-old prints
    Waterfall

FORTS AND FORTIFICATIONS
        Subdivided by adjective of nationality.
    United States

FORTUNE-TELLERS

FOSSILS
    See also Geology

FOUNTAINS

FOURTH OF JULY

FRATERNAL ORDERS

FROGS. See Amphibians

FRUIT
    Subdivided by name of fruit.

FRUIT GROWING
    Subdivided by name of fruit.
    Methods

FRUIT STUDIES

FUNGI

FURNITURE
    Subdivided by periods and also by adjective of nationality or by
    name of article of furniture:
    Adam
    American-Colonial
        Bed
        Chair
        Chest
        Cupboard
        Desk
        Highboy
        Lowboy
        Table
        Utensils
    American-Federal
    Ancient
    Art Nouveau
    Bar
    Biedemeier
    Bookcase
    Byzantine
    Chair
    Chest
    Chinese

FURNITURE (cont'd)
  Chippendale
  Czechoslovak
  Desk
  Directoire
  Duncan Phyfe
  Dutch
  Egyptian
  Elizabethan
  Empire
  English
  French Provincial
  Garden
  Gothic
  Hepplewhite
  Italian
  Jacobean
  Louis XII. See Furniture-Renaissance
  Louis XIV
  Louis XV
  Louis XVI
  Mirror
  Mission
  Norman. See Romanesque
  Porch. See Garden
  Queen Anne
  Regency. See Louis XV
  Renaissance
  Restoration. See Empire
  Rococo. See Baroque
  Romanesque
  Scandinavian
  Sheraton
  Sofa
  Swiss
  Table
  Twentieth Century-1900-1929
                  -1930-1939
                  -1940-1949
                  -1950-1959
                  -1960-1969
  Victorian
  Wicker
  William and Mary

FURS

GAMES AND AMUSEMENTS
    Billiards
    Bull fighting
    Card playing
    Checkers
    Chess
    Cockfighting
    Croquet
    Deck
    Ferris wheel
    Merry-go-round
    Olympic games
    Ping-pong
    Roller coaster
    Roulette
    Shows
        Dog
        Horse
        Ice
        Night club

GARDENING

GARDENS
    American
    Arbor
    Chinese
    English
    Formal
    French
    Furniture. _See_ Furniture-Garden
    Gate
    Greenhouses
    Hedges
    Indoors
    Italian
    Japanese
    Landscape
    Ornament
    Persian
    Plan
    Pool
    Rock
    Roof
    Seats
    Spanish
    Steps

GARDENS (cont'd)
  Terrace
  Topiary
  Wall

GAS

GEMS

GEOLOGY

GHOSTS

GIANTS

GIRL SCOUTS

GLASS
    Subdivided by adjective of nationality and the following:
    Ancient
    Architectural
    Manufacture
        See also Stained Glass

GLOBES

GOBLINS. See Brownies and Goblins

GOLD. See Metalwork; Minerals; Mining

GRAIN ELEVATORS. See Wheat

GRAINS AND GRASSES

GRANITE. See Quarrying

GRAPHS. See Drawing-Graph

GRAVES. See Cemeteries; Monuments and memorials; Sculpture-
        Greek-Grave monuments; Tombs; Tombstones

GREENHOUSES. See Gardens-Greenhouse

GREENLAND. See Islands-Greenland

GRINDSTONES

GROTESQUES

GUNS. <u>See</u> Armament

GYMNASIUMS

GYMNASTICS

GYPSIES

HABITATIONS
  Cave
  Cliff
  Hut
  Igloo
  Lake   <u>See also</u> Boathouses
  Pueblo
  Tent
  Tree

HALLOWEEN

HANDICAPPED
    <u>See also</u> Blind

HANDICRAFTS
  Basketry
  Cement
  Gesso
  Leather
  Metal
  Paper
  Soap
  Toys
  Weaving
  Wood
  Workers

HARBORS. <u>See</u> Forms of Land and Water; Wharves and Docks

HARVEST. <u>See</u> Autumn; Farm; Symbolic pictures-Harvest

HATMAKING

HEATING AND VENTILATING

HEMP

HERALDRY. <u>See</u> Coats of Arms

HOLIDAYS. See Arbor Day; Christmas; Decoration Day; Easter;
            Explorers-Columbus; Flag Day; Fourth of July;
            Halloween; May Day; New Year; Portraits-Lincoln;
            Portraits-Washington; St. Patrick's Day; Thanks-
            giving; Valentines; Veterans' Day

HOME ECONOMICS
    Care of children
    Care of house
    Clothing
    Cooking
    Home accessories
    Marketing. See Markets; Stores
    Sewing
    Washing

HOSPITALS
    Exterior
    Interior

HOTELS
    Subdivided by adjective of nationality and United States.

HOUSE PAINTER. See Occupations-House Painter

HOUSE PLANS

HOUSES-Exterior
    1900-1919
    1920-1939
    1940-1959
    1960-
    American Colonial
    American Federal
    American Historic
    Apartment
    Bermuda
    Brick
    Bungalow
    Chalet
    Cottage
    Elizabethan
    English
    French
    Georgian
    Half Timber
    Hutch
    Italian

HOUSES-Exterior (cont'd)
Log
Norman
Patio
Regency
Spanish
Stone
Stucco
Swiss
Three-family
Tudor
Two-family
Victorian
Wood

HOUSES-Interior
Subdivided by adjective of nationality and the following dates;
1890-1899, 1900-1929, 1930-1939, 1940-1949, 1950-1959, 1960-1969.
American-Colonial
-Historic
Attic
Bathroom
Bedroom
Decoration
Dining Room
Directoire
Empire
French Provincial
Game Room
Georgian
Hall and Stairway
Italian
Jacobean
Kitchen
Library
Living Room
Log
Louis XII, XIV, XV, XVI
Mexican
Nursery
Penthouse
Queen Anne
Scandinavian
Spanish
Sun Room
Tudor
Victorian

HOUSING

HUMANE SOCIETIES. See Kindness to animals

HUMOR. See Caricatures; Cartoons

HYGIENE
    Care of teeth
    Cleanliness
    Exercise
    Food
      Bread
      Cereal
      Fruit
      Milk
      Vegetable
    Fresh Air
    Infant
    Posture
    Prevention of disease
    Rest
    Skin and Hair

ICE

ICELAND. See Europe-Iceland

IDOLS. See Religions

ILLUMINATION
    Celtic
    English
    Flemish
    French
    German
    Initial
    Persian
    Modern
    Spanish

ILLUSTRATIONS
    Subdivided by name of author and title and also by the following
      headings:
    Alice in Wonderland. See Illustrations-Dodgson
    Arabian Nights
    Drama (Subdivided by author and title)
    Fairy Tales (Except for Aesop, Andersen, and La Fontaine)

ILLUSTRATIONS (cont'd)
    Legends
    Music
    Musical Plays
    Nursery Rhymes (By first line)
    Opera (By composer and title)
    Robin Hood
    Science Fiction
    Songs
    Story Telling
    Technique

ILLUSTRATORS
    Subdivided by names of illustrators.

IMMIGRATION

INDIANS
    Forest
    Northwest
    Plains
        Dwellings
        Manners and customs
    Southwest
        Dwellings
        Manners and customs
    Useful Arts
        Basketry
        Ceramics
        Textiles

INDUSTRIES. See Names of industries

INLAY. See Marquetry

INNS AND TAVERNS
    Subdivided by adjective of nationality and:
    Scenes in
    Signs

INSECTS
    Subdivided by names of insects.
    Injurious

INTARSIA. See Marquetry

INTERNATIONAL SIGNAL CODES. See Flags-Marine

INVENTIONS

IRON. See Steel and Iron

IRRIGATION

ISLANDS
> Subdivided by name of the specific island with the following ex-
> ceptions: Islands located near the mother country are classified
> under the appropriate continent and country. For example:
> Europe-Italy-Sicily.
>
> Islands are classified by group name if the individual island is not
> identified but is of a particular group and if there are so few pic-
> tures of a given island as to make separation impractical.
> Unidentifiable islands are classified under their general geographic
> area.

Azores
Bahamas (Nassau)
Barbados
Bermuda
>   Hamilton
>   St. George

Canary
Caribbean (Collective and Unidentified)
Carolines
Ceylon
Corsica
Crete
Cuba (Includes Isle of Pines)
>   Havana
>   History

Curacao
Cypress
Dominican Republic
Fiji
Formosa
Greenland
Guadeloupe
Guam See also Is. -Marianas
Haiti
Iceland
Indonesia
>   Bali
>   Manners and customs
>   People
>   Borneo

ISLANDS
  Indonesia (cont'd)
    Java
      Manners and Customs
      People
      Resources
    Sumatra
      Manners and Customs
      People
      Resources
  Jamaica
  Madagascar
  Malta
  Martinique
  New Guinea
  New Hebrides
  New Zealand
  Philippines
    History
    Manners and Customs
    People
    Resources
  Pitcairn
  Puerto Rico
    San Juan
    Manners and Customs
    People
    Resources
  Rhodes
  Samoa
  Solomon (includes Guadalcanal)
  South Seas (collective and unidentified)
  Tahiti
  Trinidad
  Virgin
  Zanzibar

ISLANDS - Classification of Major Islands
  Aleutian   see U.S. - Alaska
  Antigua   see Is. - Antigua
  Aruba   see Is. - Aruba
  Ascension   see Is. - Ascension
  Azores   see Is. - Azores
  Baffin   see Canada
  Bahamas   see Is. - Bahamas
  Balearic   see Europe-Spain
  Bali   see Is. - Indonesia-Bali
  Barbados   see Is. - Barbados
  Bermuda   see Is. - Bermuda

ISLANDS - Classification of Major Islands (cont'd)
Bimini	see	Is. -Bahamas-Bimini
Bonins	see	Is. -Bonins
Borabora	see	Is. -Society-Borabora
Borneo	see	Is. -Indonesia-Borneo
Bornholm	see	Europe-Denmark
Canary	see	Is. -Canary
Canton	see	Is. -Phoenix-Canton
Cape Verde	see	Is. -Cape Verde
Capri	see	Europe-Italy
Caribbean	see	Is. -Caribbean
Carolines	see	Is. -Carolines
Celebes	see	Is. -Indonesia-Celebes
Ceylon	see	Is. -Ceylon
Chatham	see	Is. -New Zealand-Chatham
Christmas	see	Is. -Christmas
Corfu	see	Europe-Greece
Corsica	see	Is. -Corsica
Crete	see	Is. -Crete
Cuba	see	Is. -Cuba
Curacao	see	Is. -Curacao
Cyprus	see	Is. -Cyprus
Devil's Is.	see	Is. -Devil's Is.
Dominica	see	Is. -Dominica
Dom. Rep.	see	Is. -Dominican Republic
Easter	see	Is. -Easter
Elba	see	Europe-Italy
Faeroes	see	Is. -Faeroes
Falklands	see	Is. -Falklands
Fatu Hiva	see	Is. -Marquesas-Fatu Hiva
Fayal	see	Is. -Azores-Fayal
Fiji	see	Is. -Fiji
Formosa	see	Is. -Formosa
Galapagos	see	Is. -Galapagos
Gilbert & Ellice	see	Is. -Gilbert & Ellice
Greenland	see	Is. -Greenland
Grenada	see	Is. -Grenada
Grenadines	see	Is. -Grenadines
Guadalcanal	see	Is. -Solomon-Guadalcanal
Guadeloupe	see	Is. -Guadeloupe
Guam	see	Is. -Guam
Haiti	see	Is. -Haiti
Hawaiian	see	U. S. -Hawaii
Hebrides	see	Europe-Scotland
Iceland	see	Is. -Iceland
Jamaica	see	Is. -Jamaica
Java	see	Is. -Indonesia-Java

ISLANDS - Classification of Major Islands (cont'd)

Kermadec	see	Is.-New Zealand-Kermadec
Luzon	see	Is.-Philippines-Luzon
Madagascar	see	Is.-Madagascar
Madeiras	see	Is.-Madeiras
Madura	see	Is.-Indonesia-Madura
Maldives	see	Is.-Maldives
Malta	see	Is.-Malta
Marianas	see	Is.-Marianas
Marquesas	see	Is.-Marquesas
Marshall	see	Is.-Marshall
Martinique	see	Is.-Martinique
Mauritius	see	Is.-Mauritius
Mindanao	see	Is.-Philippines-Mindanao
Moluccas	see	Is.-Indonesia-Moluccas
Moorea	see	Is.-Society-Moorea
New Caledonia	see	Is.-New Caledonia
New Guinea	see	Is.-New Guinea
New Hebrides	see	Is.-New Hebrides
New Zealand	see	Is.-New Zealand
Newfoundland	see	Canada
Nuku Hiva	see	Is.-Marquesas-Nuku Hiva
Okinawa	see	Is.-Okinawa
Orkney	see	Europe-Scotland-Orkney
Philippines	see	Is.-Philippines
Pitcairn	see	Is.-Pitcairn
Phoenix	see	Is.-Phoenix
Puerto Rico	see	Is.-Puerto Rico
Rapa	see	Is.-Rapa
Rhodes	see	Is.-Rhodes
Saba (Neth.)	see	Is.-Saba
Saint Croix	see	Is.-Virgin-St. Croix
Saint Eustatius	see	Is.-Saint Eustatius
Saint Helena	see	Is.-Saint Helena
Saint John	see	Is.-Virgin-St. John
Saint Kitts	see	Is.-Saint Kitts
Saint Lucia	see	Is.-Saint Lucia
Saint Pierre	see	Is.-Saint Pierre
Saint Thomas	see	Is.-Virgin-St. Thomas
Saint Vincent	see	Is.-Saint Vincent
Saipan	see	Is.-Marianas-Saipan
Samoa	see	Is.-Samoa
Sao Miguel	see	Is.-Azores-Sao Miguel
Sardinia	see	Europe-Italy
Shetland	see	Europe-Scotland
Sicily	see	Europe-Italy
Singapore	see	Asia-Singapore
Society	see	Is.-Society

ISLANDS - Classification of Major Islands (cont'd)
<table>
<tr><td>Solomon</td><td>see</td><td>Is. -Solomon</td></tr>
<tr><td>South Seas</td><td>see</td><td>Is. -South Seas</td></tr>
<tr><td>Sumatra</td><td>see</td><td>Is. -Indonesia-Sumatra</td></tr>
<tr><td>Suva</td><td>see</td><td>Is. -Fiji-Suva</td></tr>
<tr><td>Tahiti</td><td>see</td><td>Is. -Tahiti</td></tr>
<tr><td>Takatoa</td><td>see</td><td>Is. -Tuamotu-Takatoa</td></tr>
<tr><td>Tasmania</td><td>see</td><td>Australia-Tasmania</td></tr>
<tr><td>Tikopia</td><td>see</td><td>Is. -Tikopia</td></tr>
<tr><td>Timor</td><td>see</td><td>Is. -Indonesia-Timor</td></tr>
<tr><td>Tonga</td><td>see</td><td>Is. -Tonga</td></tr>
<tr><td>Trinidad</td><td>see</td><td>Is. -Trinidad</td></tr>
<tr><td>Tuamotu</td><td>see</td><td>Is. -Tuamotu</td></tr>
<tr><td>Virgin</td><td>see</td><td>Is. -Virgin</td></tr>
<tr><td>Yap</td><td>See also</td><td>Islands-Carolines</td></tr>
<tr><td>Zanzibar</td><td>see</td><td>Is. -Zanzibar</td></tr>
</table>

IVORY

JADE

JANITOR. See Occupations-Janitor

JAPANESE PRINTS. See Art-Japanese

JEWELRY
    Subdivided by adjective of nationality and also by the following:
    American Indian
    Bag
    Le Bijou
    Bracelet and Earring
    Buckle
    Cuff Button
    Hair Ornament
    History
    Lorgnette
    Manufacture
    Necklace and Pendant
    Pin
    Ring
    Watch

JEWELRY-ENGRAVING. See Lettering-Engraved

JEWS. See Asia-Israel; Asia-Palestine; Immigration; Religions-
          Judaic; United States-People

JUNGLE

KERAMICS. See Ceramics

KINDNESS TO ANIMALS

KITES. See Wind

KNIGHTHOOD. See Armor; Middle Ages

KU KLUX KLAN

LABOR
See also Child Labor

LABORATORIES

LACE
Subdivided by adjective of nationality and the following:
Making

LACQUER

LAKE DWELLERS. See Boathouses; Habitations-Lake; Races-
Prehistoric

LAMPS. See Lighting

LANDSCAPE GARDENING. See Gardens-Landscape

LANDSCAPES

LANTERNS. See Lighting

LAWYER. See Occupations-Lawyer

LEAGUE OF NATIONS

LEATHER
-Historic

LETTERING
Block
Chinese
Composition
Engraved
Fancy
Gothic
Initial
Italics and script

LETTERING (cont'd)
  Japanese
  Monogram
  Renaissance
  Roman
  Showcard

LIBRARIES
  Ancient
  Australian
  Canadian
  English and Scotch
  French
  German
  Italian
  Russian
  South American
  United States
    Subdivided by names of states.

LIFE SAVING

LIGHTHOUSES

LIGHTING
    See also Searchlights

LIGHTNING
    For Artificial lightning See Electricity

LINEN

LINOLEUM

LITHOGRAPHERS
    Subdivided by names of artists including Currier & Ives.
  Currier & Ives
    The American scene
    Boats and ships
    Camping, fishing and hunting
    Farm scene
    Life on the prairie
    Racing and trotting
    Railroad scene
    Seasons

LITHOGRAPHY

LOCKS AND KEYS. See Metalwork-Door fittings

LOOMS. See Spinning and weaving

LUMBERING

MACHINERY
    Construction
    Cranes and Shovels
    Historic
    In art
    Parts of
    Presses
    Turbines and Steam Generators
    Welding
        See also Building Construction; Farm-Machinery; Physics-
           Simple Machines

MADONNAS - Classified by the name of the artist

MADONNAS IN SCULPTURE

MAGAZINE COVERS

MANUSCRIPTS
    Ancient
    Artists
    Historic
    Historic-American
    Music
    Writers

MAPLE SUGAR. See Sugar-Maple

MAPS
    Decorative
    Historic
    Making or projection
        See also Maps under the heading of each country and by the
           separate states of the United States. Animal maps
           are classified under: Animals-Maps-by continent

MARBLE

MARINAS

MARINE CORPS. See Navy-U.S.-Marine Corps

MARINE STUDIES

MARIONETTES

MARKETS
  See also Fairs; Stores-Food

MARQUETRY

MASKS

MASON. See Occupations-Mason

MATHEMATICS

MAY DAY

MEAT
  See also Food-Meat

MEDALS
          -U.S.
          -U.S.-War

MEDICINE
          -History
  See also Name of physician or scientist under Portraits; Diseases;
            First aid; Plants-Medicinal; Surgery; X-ray

MEMORIAL DAY. See Decoration Day

MEMORIALS. See Monuments and Memorials; Tablets; Tombs

MENTAL HEALTH

MERCHANT MARINE

MERMAIDS

MERRY-GO-ROUND. See Games and amusements-Merry-go-round

METAL INDUSTRY

METALWORK
  Subdivided by adjective of nationality and by the following:
  American
  Architectural
  Art of Making

METALWORK (cont'd)
Cup
Door Fittings
Ecclesiastical
English
Engraved
Fire Irons
French
Furniture-Hardware
German
Home Accessories
Italian
Lighting Fixtures
Medieval
Renaissance
South American
Tableware
Trophies

METEOROLOGY. See Astronomy; Clouds; Rain; Rainbow; Storms;
                                Weather; Wind

MEXICO
Subdivided by name of city and by the following:
History
          -Ancient
Lakes
Maps
Mountains
Rivers

MICROSCOPES

MIDDLE AGES
See also   Armor; Castles; Cathedrals; Costume-Medieval;
                   Crusades; Metalwork-Medieval; Mosaics-Medieval;
                   Sculpture-Medieval

MILLS

MINER. See Mining; Occupations-Miner

MINERALS
See also   Aluminum; Gems; Geology; Jade; Marble; Mining;
                   Nitrate; Quarrying; Salt; Sand, etcetera

MINIATURES

MINING
    Subdivided by name of mineral.

MIRAGE

MIRRORS. See Furniture-Mirror

MISSIONS
    Foreign
    United States
        California
        California-Santa Barbara

MODELS

MONASTERIES
    Scenes in

MONUMENTS AND MEMORIALS
    Subdivided by adjective of nationality and the following:
    New Jersey
    United States

MOSAICS
    Antioch
    Byzantine-Istanbul
            -Ravenna
    Design
    Early Christian
    Greek
    Medieval
    Renaissance
    Roman
    Sicilian-Monreale
            -Palermo

MOSQUES

MOSS. See Plants

MOTELS

MOTHER'S DAY. See Family; Madonnas; Painters-Whistler

MOUNTAIN CLIMBING. See Sports

MOVING PICTURES
Subdivided alphabetically by name of film and the following:
Awards
Historic
Technique
Westerns

MUMMIES. See Antiquities-Egyptian

MUNICIPAL ART. See City Planning

MUNICIPAL BUILDINGS. See City Halls; Court Houses; Customs
Houses; Police Stations; Post Offices;
Prisons; State Houses

MURAL PAINTING. See Painting-Mural

MUSEUMS
Subdivided by adjective of nationality and U.S., and further by
name of museum and the following:
Design
Exhibitions

MUSIC-MAPS

MUSICAL INSTRUMENTS
Subdivided by name of instrument and by the following:
Ancient
Collective
In art

MUSICIANS
Bands
Ensembles
In art
Orchestras
Organists
Pianists

MYTHOLOGY
Celtic
East Indian
Egyptian
Greek and Roman
Subdivided by name of mythological characters using Roman
names for Greek and Roman deities or heroes.
Japanese

MYTHOLOGY (cont'd)
   Norse and German
      Subdivided by names of mythological characters using Norse
      names when classifying.

NARCOTICS. See Crime and Criminology; Diseases; Medicine; Plants

N.A.T.O.

NAVIGATION

NAVY
   English
   French
   German
   Japanese
   United States
      Aircraft Carrier
      Airplane
      Battleship
      Coast Guard. See Coast Guard
      Crew
      Cruiser
      Destroyer
      Historic
         Obsolete ships
      Hospital Ships
      Marine Corps
      Marine Corps-European War 1914-18
                 -Historic
                 -Korea
                 -Training
                 -Vietnam
                 -World War II
      Small craft
      Submarine
      Torpedo
      Training
      Yards

NEEDLEWORK
   Applique
   Beadwork
   Church
   Crochet
   Cross-stitch

NEEDLEWORK (cont'd)
  Embroidery
    Fashions in
    National - Subdivided by adjective of nationality.
    Patterns
    Picture
  Knitting
  Monogram
  Needlepoint
  Pattern
  Quilt and Bedspread
  Sampler

NEGROES. See United States-People; United States-Plantation Life;
      and Portraits of Negro individuals

NEW ENGLAND VILLAGE LIFE. See United States-Village Life

NEW JERSEY - For geography of New Jersey, see United States-
      New Jersey.
  Armed forces
  Art
  Churches
  Forts
  History
    1660-1775
    1776-1790
    1791-1825
    1826-1850
    1851-1900
    1901-1940
    1941
  Houses
  Indians
  Inns and Taverns
  Mills
  Mines
  Monuments and Memorials
  Parks
  Post Offices
  Schools

NEW YEAR

NEWARK
  Airport
  Bay
  Bird's-eye views

NEWARK (cont'd)
  Bridges
  Buildings
      Armory
      Banks
      Baths
      City Hall
      Court House
      Institutions
      Insurance
      Jail
      Library
      Museum
      Office
      Post Office
      Railroad Stations
      Theatres and Halls
  Celebrations
  Cemeteries
  Churches
  Club Houses
  Colleges
  Fire Department
  Government
  Historic
      Colonial
      Revolution 1765-1787
      By decade from 1790 to present day
  Homes
  Hospitals
  Hotels
  Industries
      Subdivided by name.
  Maps
  Markets
  Meadows
  Medals
  Newspapers
  Parks
      Subdivided by name.
  Passaic River
  People
  Playgrounds
  Police Department
  Port Newark
  Portraits
      Subdivided by name.
  Posters

NEWARK (cont'd)
 Schools
   -Public
 Sculpture
  Subdivided by sculptor and statue.
 Stores
 Streets
 Tablets
 Theatres
 Transportation
 Trees
 Water Supply

NEWFOUNDLAND. See Canada

NEWSBOYS. See Occupation-Newsboys

NEWSPAPERS. See Communication-Newspaper

NIGHT

NITRATE

NUMISMATICS. See Coins; Medals

NURSING. See Occupations-Nurse; Red Cross; Surgery

NUTS

OBSERVATORIES

OCCUPATIONS
 Subdivided by the name of the occupation and:
 Collective

OCEAN. See Forms of land and Water-Ocean; Marine Studies;
   Oceanography; Painters-Homer, Israels, Waugh,
   etcetera; Seashore; U.S.-Coast Line

OCEANOGRAPHY

OFFICES

OIL

OIL PAINTING STUDIES. See Color Studies; Flower Studies; Fruit
        Studies; Landscapes; Marine Studies;
        Painters; Painting-Oil; Painting-Still
        life

OLD AGE

OLYMPIC GAMES. See Games and amusements–Olympic games

OPERA HOUSES

OPTICAL ILLUSIONS
     See also Mirage

OPTICAL INSTRUMENTS

ORGAN GRINDER

ORPHANS. See Social settlement

PAGEANTS

PAINTER. See Occupations–Artist; Occupations–House painter

PAINTERS
     Subdivided by name of painter and also by title or subject for
     major artists as for Rembrandt below.

PAINTERS–REMBRANDT
     Anatomy Lesson
     Aristotle Contemplating the Bust of Homer
     Jacob Blessing the Sons of Joseph
     Lady with a Pink
     Landscapes
     Lucretia
     Night Watch
     Noble Slav
     Old Woman Cutting her Nails
     Portraits–Men
     Portraits–Women
     Religious Paintings
     Saskia
     Self-Portraits
     Supper at Emmaus
     Syndics
     Titus
     Young Painter

PAINTING
     Abstract
     American
     American Indian
     Chinese

PAINTING (cont'd)
    Dutch
    East Indian
    English
    Etruscan
    Figure
    Finger
    Flemish
    Flowers
       See also Flower Studies
    French
    Fresco
    Genre
    German
    Italian
    Japanese
    Marine. See Marine Studies
    Mural
       Subdivided by nationality.
    Non-Objective
    Oil
    Persian
    Polish
    Portrait
    Russian
    Scandinavian
    South American
    Spanish
    Still Life
    Surrealism
    Water Color
    World War, 1939-1945

PALACES
    Subdivided by adjective of nationality and further by name of
    palace.

PANAMA. See Canals; Central America

PANELS. See Design-Panel

PAPER

PAPER CUTTING

PAPER MAKING

PARACHUTES. See Transportation-Air-Plane-Parachute; Army-U.S.-
    Parachute and Airborne troops

PARADES
>   See also Circus-Parades; Festivals; Floats

PARKS
>   See also City planning-Parks and squares

PARTIES

PASSION PLAY

PEARL FISHING
>   See also Pearls

PEARLS
>   See also Pearl fishing

PEAT

PEDDLER. See Occupations-Peddler

PERFUME
>   See also Advertising-Perfume

PEWTER. See Metalwork

PHONOGRAPH RECORD COVERS. See Design-Phonograph record
>   covers

PHOTO-MECHANICAL PROCESSES. See Etching processes; Litho-
>   graphy; Printing processes

PHOTOGRAPHERS
>   Subdivided by name of photographer.

PHOTOGRAPHY
>   Aerial
>   Color
>   Equipment
>   Historic
>   Motion. See Moving Pictures-Technique
>   Science

PHYSICS
>   Electricity
>   Heat
>   Historic
>   Light
>   Magnetism

PHYSICS (cont'd)
   Simple Machines
      See also Machinery
   Sound
      See also Communication; Electricity; Lighting; Machinery; Micro-
         scopes; Weights and Measures; X-ray

PHYSIOLOGY
   Alimentary Canal
   Ear
   Eye
   Hand
   Heart
   Muscles
   Skeleton

PICNICS

PILGRIMS. See Costume-American-Colonial; Thanksgiving; U.S.
        History-Colonization

PILOT. See Navigation; Occupations-Pilot

PIPES. See Musical Instruments; Sewers; Tobacco Pipes

PIRATES

PLANTATION LIFE. See Cotton; U.S.-Plantation Life

PLANTS
   Subdivided by name of plant and:
   Collective
   Injurious
   Medicinal

PLASTICS

PLAYGROUNDS. See City Planning

PLAYHOUSES

PLUMBER. See Occupations-Plumber

POLAR REGIONS
   Maps

POLICEMAN. See Occupations-Policeman; Police Departments

POLICE DEPARTMENTS

POLLUTION

PONY EXPRESS. See Communication-Postal Service

PORCELAIN. See Ceramics

PORCH. See Architectural Details-Porch

PORTRAITS
    Subdivided by name of the person with special headings as listed.
    Franklin (By number)
    Lincoln (By number)
    Popes
    Presidents (For collective portraits)
    Roosevelt, F. D. (By number)
    Shakespeare (By number)
    Washington, George (By number)

PORTRAITS-FRANKLIN
    1 Birthplace and Youth
    2 Family
    3 Inventor
    4 Statesman
    5 Portraits and Statues
    6 Printer
    7 Miscellaneous

PORTRAITS-LINCOLN
    1 Early Days
    2 Homes
    3 Family
    4 Portraits
    4a Statues
    5 Presidency
    6 Death
    7 Letters, speeches, portraits of contemporaries

PORTRAITS-POPES

PORTRAITS-PRESIDENTS (collective only)

PORTRAITS-ROOSEVELT, F. D.
    1 Youth
    2 Home
    3 Family
    4 Family-Mother

PORTRAITS-ROOSEVELT, F.D. (cont'd)
  5 Family-Wife
  6 Portraits
  7 Career

PORTRAITS-SHAKESPEARE
  1 Portraits
  2 Homes
  3 Hathaway Cottage
  4 Stratford
  5 Miscellaneous

PORTRAITS-WASHINGTON, GEORGE
  1 Childhood
  2 Youth
  3 Homes
  4 Family
  5 Wife
  6 Mother
  7 Portraits
  7a Statues
  8 Portraits, Stuart
  9 Portraits, Trumbull
  10 War
  11 Crossing the Delaware
  12 Valley Forge
  13 Lafayette
  14 Presidency
  15 Last Days
  15a Last Springtime
  15b Last Birthday
  16 Miscellaneous

POST OFFICES

POSTAGE STAMPS
    Classified by nationality

POSTERS
  Citizenship
  Designers (by name)
  Education and School
  Historic
  Museums and Galleries
  Travel
  War
  War-Europe
    See also Conservation; Fire Prevention; Hygiene-Cleanliness;
       Safety-Posters

POSTMAN. See Occupations-Postman

POTTERY. See Ceramics

POULTRY. See Farm-Animals

PRINTING
  Advertising-Pamphlets
  American
  American-Franklin
  Announcements
  Broadsides
  Calendars
  Color-Processes
  Dedications, Indexes, Prefaces
  Diplomas and certificates
  Firms-American
        English
        French
        German
  Head and Tail Pieces
  History
  House Organs
  Initial
  Layout
  Letterhead
  Machinery (Including presses)
  Marks
  Menus
  Mottoes
  Ornament
  Portraits
  Processes-Collotype
  Processes-Photogravure
  Title Pages
  Typefaces
  Type Page

PRISONS

PROHIBITION. See U.S. History-1921-1929

PUBLIC BATHS

PUBLIC BUILDINGS. See Asylums and Almshouses; Banks; Business
                   buildings; City Halls; Court Houses; Hospitals;
                   Libraries; Museums; Police stations; Post
                   offices; Prisons; Public baths; Schools;
                   State Houses

SUBJECT HEADINGS 75

PUMPS. See Machinery; Physics-Simple machinery; Water Supply

PUNISHMENTS

PUPPETS. See Marionettes

PURITANS. See Costume-American-Colonial; Thanksgiving; U.S.
  History-Colonization-Massachusetts

PUTTI (Figures of nude Cupidlike children much used in decorative
  painting and sculpture).

QUAKERS. See Religions-Christian-Quaker; U.S. History-
  Colonization-Pennsylvania

QUARRYING

QUININE. See Plants-Medicinal

RACES
  Black
  Brown
  Collective
  Prehistoric
    See also Animals-Prehistoric; Habitations
  Red
  White
  Yellow

RACING. See Sports-Racing-Auto; Sports-Racing-Dog; Sports-
  Racing-Horse

RADIO. See Communication-Radio

RADIUM

RAILROAD STATIONS

RAILROADS. See Transportation-Land-Rail

RAILROAD-WRECKS. See Wrecks-Land

RAIN

RAINBOW

RANCHES. See Stock Raising; U.S.-Western Life

RAYON

REBUS. See Writing-Rebus

RED CROSS

RELIGIONS
    Buddhist
    Christian
        Amish
        Catholic
        Eastern Orthodox
        Mennonite
        Mormon
        Protestant
        Quaker
        Shaker
    Confucian
    Hinduism
    Judaism
    Mohammedan

RENDERING
    Architectural
        See also Drawing-Architectural
    Cityscape
    Interior

REPTILES
    Alligator
    Crocodile
    Lizard
    Snake
    Turtle

RESTAURANTS AND CAFES
        See also Games and amusements-Shows-Night club

RICE

RIDING. See Sports

ROADS AND VIADUCTS
        See also Streets

ROBOTS. See Illustrations-Science fiction

ROCKETS. See Armament-Missiles and rockets

ROCKS. See Geology; Minerals

ROME-HISTORY
    754-510 B. C. -Kingdom
    510-31 B. C. -Republic
    31 B. C. -284 A. D. -Early Empire
    284 A. D. -476 A. D. -Late Empire
    476-1453-Byzantine Empire
    Manners and Customs
    Portraits
        See also Europe-Italy-Rome

ROPE

ROWING. See Sports-Boating-Row

ROYALTY
    See also Crowns; Thrones; Subdivision History under name of
        country

RUBBER
    Synthetic

RUGS
    American
    Caucasian
    Chinese
    From Paintings
    Khilim
    Manufacture
    Persian
    Turkish
    Turkoman
    Twentieth Century

RUINS. See Antiquities

SAFETY
    Adult
    Children
    Posters
        See also Life Saving

SAILING. See Sports-Boating-Sail; Transportation-Water-Sail

SAILOR. See Costume-Naval; Navy; Occupations-Sailor

SAINT PATRICK'S DAY

SAINTS
>   Subdivided by name of the saint.
>   See also Saint Patrick's Day; Valentines

SALT

SALVATION ARMY

SAND

SCALES. See Weights and Measures

SCHOOLS
>   Art and Music
>   English
>   Foreign
>   Historic
>   Kindergarten
>   Military
>   Music. See Schools-Art and Music
>   Private
>   Public-Exterior
>   -Interior
>   Rural
>   Special
>   Teaching Aids
>   Technical and Professional

SCORPIONS

SCREENS

SCULPTORS
>   Subdivided by name of sculptor and further by title of work by
>   Michelangelo.

SCULPTORS-MICHELANGELO
>   David
>   Deposition
>   Madonna
>   Medici Tombs
>   Moses
>   Pieta
>   Slave

SCULPTURE
>   Subdivided by name of statue and by nationality when not identi-
>   fied by the following headings:

SCULPTURE (cont'd)
    Abstract
    African
    Animal
    Architectural
    Baroque
    East Indian
    Egyptian
    Etruscan
    Figure
    Gothic
    Greek
        Archaic
        Fifth century
        Fourth century
        Grave monuments
        Parthenon
    Hellenistic
    Mayan
    Medieval
    Mobile and stabile
    Oceanic
    Paper
    Primary structures
    Primitive
    Processes
    Renaissance
    Roman
        Portraits
    Romanesque
    Venus

SEA LIFE

SEA WALLS

SEA WEED. See Design-Sea Life; Sea Life

SEALS
    Christmas
    City
    College
    State

SEARCHLIGHTS

SEASHORE

SEASONS. See Name of Season

SEEDS

SEVEN WONDERS OF THE WORLD

SEWERS

SHADOW PICTURES. See Silhouettes

SHALE. See Geology

SHELL FISH

SHELLS
    See also Snails

SHELTERS. See Air Raid Shelters; Habitations

SHIP BUILDING

SHIPS. See Navy; Transportation-Water

SHIPWRECKS. See Wrecks-Water

SHOEMAKER. See Occupations-Cobbler; Shoemaking

SHOEMAKING

SHOES. See Costume-Accessories-Shoes; Occupations-Cobbler;
        Shoemaking

SHRINES. See Religions; Temples

SIGNBOARDS
    See also Inns and Taverns

SIGN PAINTING

SILHOUETTES
   Children
   Portraits

SILK

SILK SCREEN PRINTING

SKATING. See Sports

SKELETONS. See Physiology-Skeleton

SKULLS. See Physiology-Skeleton

SLAVERY. See U.S. History-Civil War; U.S. Plantation Life

SLUMS. See City Planning-Slums

SNAILS

SNAKE CHARMERS. See Asia-India-Manners and Customs

SNOW CRYSTALS. See Winter

SNUFF BOXES

SOAP

SOCIAL SETTLEMENT
      See also Asylums and Almhouses; Child labor; City planning;
                  Old Age

SOUTH AMERICA
      Subdivided by name of the country and also by the following:
      Andes
      History
      Incas
      Llanos
      Manners and Customs
      Maps
      Pampas
      People
      Resources
      Rivers
      Selvas

SPACE. See Astronomy-Satellites; Costume-Space; Illustrations-
            Science fiction; Transportation-Space

SPECTRUM. See Physics

SPICES. See Plants

SPIDERS

SPINNING AND WEAVING

SPONGES

SPORTS
    Aquaplaning
    Archery
    Baseball
    Basketball
    Bicycling
    Boating
        Canoe
        Motor
        Row
        Sail
        Yacht
    Bowling
    Boxing
    Coasting
        Sled
        Toboggan
    Cricket
    Deck Tennis
    Diving
        See also Diving
    Falconry
    Fencing
    Fishing
    Football
    Golf
    Hockey
        Field
        Ice
    Hunting
    Ice-Boating
    In art
    Jujitsu
    Mountain climbing
    Polo
    Racing
        Auto
        Dog
        Horse
    Riding
    Skating
        Ice
        Roller
    Skiing
    Skydiving
    Snow Shoeing
    Surfing
    Swimming

SPORTS (cont'd)
  Tennis
  Track and Field
  Tobogganing. See Sports-Coasting-Toboggan
  Volley Ball
  Water Skiing
  Weight Lifting
  Wrestling
    See also Gymnastics

SPRING

STADIA

STAGE COACHES. See Transportation-Land-Coach

STAINED GLASS
    Subdivided by adjective of nationality and the following:
  Design
  Making

STAMPS. See Postage Stamps

STATE HOUSES

STATUES. See Monuments and Memorials; Portraits; Sculptors;
           Sculpture

STEEL AND IRON
  Foreign
  Historic
  Use of

STENCILS

STILL LIFE. See Painting-Still Life

STOCK RAISING
    See also Animals-Cattle; Farm; U.S.-Western Life

STONE CARVING. See Carving-Stone

STORES
  Clothing
  Country
  Department
  Drug

STORES (cont'd)
    Food
        See also Markets
    Historic
    Window

STORMS
        See also Lightning; Rain; Weather; Wind

STOVES. See Heating and Ventilating; Home economics-Cooking;
              Houses-Interior-Kitchen

STREETS
    City
    Village
        See also Roads and Viaducts

STRIKES

STUDIOS

SUGAR
    Beet
    Cane
    Maple

SUMMER

SUMMER HOUSES

SUN DIALS. See Clocks and Watches

SUNRISE

SUNSET

SURGERY

SWIMMING. See Sports

SWIMMING POOLS

SWITCHBOARDS. See Communication-Telephone

SWORDS. See Armament-Hand weapon-Sword

SYMBOLIC PICTURES
    Abundance
    Agriculture

SYMBOLIC PICTURES (cont'd)
Alphabet
Architecture
Art
Arts and Sciences
Aspiration
Astrology
Astronomy
Avarice
Beauty
Birth
Charity
Chemical Elements
Church
City Life
Civilization
Commerce
Communication
Conditions and States
Continents
Countries
    Subdivided by country.
Courage
Dance
Daybreak
Days of the Week
Death
Disease
Divinations
Drama
Drink
Earth
Education
Electricity
Elements
Emotion
    Subdivided by emotion.
Energy
Faith
Fame
Figure
Fortune
Freedom
Gardening
Good
Habit
Happiness
Harmony

SYMBOLIC PICTURES (cont'd)
    Harvest
    Health
    Heaven
    Hell
    Heraldry
    Heroism
    History
    Holidays
    Honesty
    Hope
    Hunger
    Immortality
    Indolence
    Industries
    Industry
    Innocence
    Jealousy
    Justice
    Knowledge
    Labor
    Law
    Liberty
    Life
    Light
    Literature
    Love
    Loyalty
    Luck
    Magic
    Medicine
    Melancholy
    Memory
    Mercy
    Muses
    Music
    Mythology
    Nature
    Night
    Old Age
    Painting and Sculpture
    Patriotism
    Peace
    Personifications
    Philosophy
    Physics
    Play
    Pleasure

SYMBOLIC PICTURES (cont'd)
    Plenty
    Poetry
    Politics
    Poverty
    Power
    Prayer
    Progress
    Purity
    Qualities and Virtues
    Religions
    Sadness
    Safety
    Satan
    Satire
    Science
    Seasons
    Senses
    Sensuality
    Silence
    Simplicity
    Sleep
    Speed
    Sports
    Temptation
    Time
    Trades
    Travel
    Truth
    Universe
    Vanity
    Vices
    Victory
    Virtue
    War
    Wealth
    Wine
    Wisdom
    Wonder
    Youth

SYNAGOGUES

SYNTHETICS
    See also Plastics; Rayon

TABLE DECORATION
    See also Home Economics; Houses-Interior-Dining Room

TABLETS
  Commercial
  Memorial

TAILOR. See Occupations-Tailor

TAPESTRIES
  Bayeaux Tapestry
  Brussels
  Coptic
  English
  Flemish
  French
  Italian

TAPIOCA. See Food

TATTOOING

TAVERNS. See Inns and Taverns

TAXIDERMY

TEA

TEACHER. See Occupation-Teacher; Schools

TEEN-AGERS

TELEGRAPH. See Communication-Telegraph

TELEPHONE. See Communication-Telephone

TELESCOPES
    See also Astronomy; Observatories; Optical instruments

TEMPLES
  Chaldean
  Chinese
  East Indian
  Egyptian
  Greek
  Japanese
  Roman

TEXTILE INDUSTRY

TEXTILES. See Cotton; Design-Textiles; Linen; Rayon; Silk;
               Synthetics; Wool

THANKSGIVING

THEATER
    Actors
    Backstage
    Exterior
    Historic
        English
        English-Elizabethan
        French
        Greek and Roman
        Italian
        United States
    Interior
    Oriental
    Playbills
    Stage Settings
        See also Costume-Stage; Illustrations-Drama; Illustrations-
           Musical Plays

THRIFT

THRONES
    See also Royalty

TIDES. See Astronomy; Seashore; Weather

TILES
    Decorative
    Historic

TOBACCO
    Pipes
    Uses of

TOMBS
    Ancient
    Eighteenth Century
    Medieval
    Oriental
    Renaissance

TOMBSTONES

TOOLS

TOTEM POLES

TOURNAMENTS. See Armor; Illustrations-Scott; Illustrations-
          Tennyson; Middle Ages

TOYS AND DOLLS

TRACTORS. See Farm-Machinery

TRADE MARKS

TRAMPS

TRANSPORTATION-AIR
   Autogiro
   Balloon
            -Historic
   Dirigible
   Glider
   Helicopter
   Historic
   Jet
   Plane-One engine
            -Two engines
            -Three engines
            -Four engines
            -Six engines
            -Historic
            -Interiors
            -Parachute
            -Plans
            -Seaplane
   Rocket

TRANSPORTATION-LAND
   Animal
   Automobile
      Foreign
      Historic-19th Century
            -1900-1910
            -1911-1920
            -1921-1930
            -1931-1940
            -1941-1950
            -1951-1960
            -1961-
            -Collective
   Bus
   Carriage
   Cart

TRANSPORTATION-LAND (cont'd)
Coach
Human
Litter
Motorcycle
Prairie Schooner
Rail
Coach
Engines
Freight
Historic
Interiors
Signals
Yards
Sedan Chair
Sled
Trolley
Truck

TRANSPORTATION-SPACE
Astronauts
Capsules
Excursion Modules
Launching
Re-Entry
Research and Testing
See also Costume-Space; Illustrations-Science Fiction

TRANSPORTATION-WATER
Barge
Collective
Ferry
Freighter and cargo
Harbor and coastal
Historic (by adjective of nationality and the following)
Historic-American-Cleremont
-Clipper Ships
-Constitution
-Mayflower I and II
-Mississippi Steamboats
-Niagara
-Savannah
Houseboat
Liner-Exterior
-Exterior and Interior
-Interior
Riverboat

TRANSPORTATION-WATER (cont'd)
   Sail (Note: Other than Clipper Ships and Yachts)
   Tug

TREES
      Subdivided by name of tree and the following:
   Blossoms
   Collective
   Evergreen
   Historic
   Leaf

TUBERCULOSIS. See Diseases

TUNNELS

TURPENTINE

TYPEWRITERS

UNIDENTIFIED FLYING OBJECTS

UNIFORMS. See Army; Costume-Military; Costume-Naval; Navy; and
            History Classification for separate nations

UNITED NATIONS
   Buildings-Exterior
            -Interior
   Delegates
   Economic and Social Council
   General Assembly
   International Court of Justice
   International Trusteeship Council
   Security Council

UNITED STATES
      Subdivided by name of state and city, except N.Y. City which is
      filed after New York state. In addition, each state may be class-
      ified by the following headings: History; Manners and customs;
      Maps; People; Resources. See Alaska below.
   Alaska
      Juneau
      Ketchikan
      Mountains
      Sitka
      History
      Manners and Customs
      Maps

UNITED STATES
   Alaska (cont'd)
      People
      Resources
   Coast Line
   District of Columbia - Washington
      Bird's-eye views
      Buildings - Subdivided by name of building.
      Historic
      Maps
      Monuments and memorials - Subdivided by name of monument or
                                memorial.
   Lakes
   Maps
   Mountains
   National Parks   (National History Parks are entered under U. S. -
                History or by State).
      Acadia
      Big Bend
      Bryce Canyon
      Carlsbad Caverns
      Crater Lake
      Everglades
      Glacier
         Blackfeet Indians
         Lakes
         Waterfalls
         Wild Life
      Grand Canyon
      Grand Teton
      Great Smoky Mountains
      Hawaii
      Hot Springs
      Isle Royale
      Kings Canyon
      Lassen Volcanic
      Mammoth Cave
      Mesa Verde
      Mount McKinley
      Mount Rainier
      Olympic
      Platt
      Rocky Mountain
      Sequoia
      Shenandoah
      Virgin Islands
      Wind Cave

UNITED STATES
    National Parks (cont'd)
        Yellowstone
            Canyons
            Geysers
            Hot Springs
            Rivers
            Waterfalls
            Wild Life
        Yosemite
            El Capital
            Half Dome
            Trees
            Waterfalls
        Zion

New Jersey
    See also New Jersey

New York City
    Bay
    Bay-Historic
    Bird's-eye views
    Bridges
    Bronx
    Brooklyn
    Buildings
        Subdivided by name of building and the following:
        Banks
        Carnegie Hall
        City Hall
        Colosseum
        Customs House
        Empire State
        Fuller
        Historic
        Insurance
        Libraries
        Madison Square Garden
        Rockefeller Center
        Woolworth
    Changing Scene
    Chinatown
    Churches
    Clubhouses
    Coney Island
    Greenwich Village
    Harlem

UNITED STATES
  New York City (cont'd)
    Historic
      1600's
      1700's
      1800-1850
      1851-1900
      1901-1910
      1911-1920
      1921-1930
      1931-1940
      1941-1960
      1961-
    Homes
    Hospitals
    Hotels
    Houses-Historic
    Industries
    Lincoln Center
    Maps
    Monuments
    Museums
    Parades
    Parks
    Parks-Historic
    People
    Playgrounds
    Port Authority
    Queens
    Railroad Stations
    Schools
    Sculpture
    Staten Island
    Statue of Liberty
    Stock Exchange
    Stores
    Street Scenes
    Streets
    Streets-Historic
    Theaters
    Transportation

  Niagara Falls
    Color
    Historic
    Winter scenes

  Rivers

UNITED STATES (cont'd)
Virginia-Williamsburg. See Art-American-Restoration-Williamsburg

UNITED STATES-GOVERNMENT
Charts
Documents
Elections and Voting
Executive
Judicial
Legislative

UNITED STATES-HISTORY
to 1607 - Pre-Colonization
1607-1765 Colonization Subdivided by states.
Colonial Massachusetts is subdivided by number as follows:
1 Embarkation and Landing
2 Mayflower and Mayflower Compact
3 Plymouth Rock
4 John Eliot
John Winthrop
Mrs. Anne Pollard
Rev. John Cotton
5 Miles Standish
6 Full weight and quality
The challenge answered
They kept faith
7 Exiles (Ferris)
Departure of the Mayflower (Bayes)
Return of the Mayflower (Ferris)
8 Furniture and Utensils
Houses
9 Punishments
Wenlock Christison defying the court
10 Boughton paintings:
Pilgrim Exiles
Pilgrims going to church
Puritans going to church
Return of the Mayflower
11 Miscellaneous

1607-1765-Colonization
Pre-Revolutionary Wars

1765-1787-Revolution
Opening events-1765-1775
Boston Massacre
Boston Tea Party

UNITED STATES-HISTORY
    Opening Events-1765-1775 (cont'd)
      Bunker Hill
      Concord
      Continental Congress
      Four intolerable acts
      General Gage
      George III
      Lexington
      Minute Men
      Parson's Cause
      Patrick Henry (Virginia Resolution)
      Paul Revere
      Quebec Act
      Spirit of '76
      Stamp Act
      The Gaspee
      Ticonderoga
      Townshend Acts
      William Pitt

    Campaigns - 1776-1787
      Anthony Wayne
      Battle of Camden
      Battle of Cowpens
      Battle of King's Mountain
      Benedict Arnold
      Bennington
      Brandywine
      Brooklyn Heights
      Burgoyne
      Clark
      Crossing the Delaware
      Evacuation of Boston
      Foreign Aid
      Fort Moultrie
      Frontier warfare
      Germantown
      General Marion
      John Jay
      John Paul Jones
      Long Island
      Major Andre
      Monmouth
      Morristown
      Naval warfare
      Oriskany
      Princeton

UNITED STATES-HISTORY
    Campaigns - 1776-1787 (cont'd)
        Putnam's escape
        Recapture of Ticonderoga
        Saratoga
        Savannah
        Treaty of Peace
        Valley Forge
        Washington takes command of army
        White Plains
        Wyoming Massacre
        Yorktown

    Foundation of government
        Annapolis convention
        Articles of Confederation
        Constitution
        Declaration of Independence 1776
        Liberty Bell

    1787-1860-Union and Development
        First Congress, 1789
        War with the Tripoli Pirates (1801-1805)
        Westward Expansion
            Crossing Mountains, Rivers
            Crossing the Plains
            Forts
            Gold Rush
            Hunters and traders
            Indians
            Louisiana Purchase
            Pioneer Homes
            Railroads
        War of 1812
        War with Mexico

    1861-1865-Civil War
        Armaments
        Battlefields
        Battles
            Subdivided alphabetically by location and by date if more than
            one battle at the same location.
        Civilian scenes
        Confederacy
        Espionage
        Forts
        Harper's Weekly and Leslie's Illustrated Newspaper
        Medical service (includes hospitals)

UNITED STATES-HISTORY
  1861-1865-Civil War (cont'd)
    Naval craft
    Naval engagements
    Parades and reviews
    Portraits - Arranged alphabetically
    Prisons and prisoners
    Surrender
    Troops
      Confederate
      Union

  1865-1898-Reconstruction

  1898-1900-Spanish-American War

  1898-1920

  1917-1921-European War

  1921-1929

  1930 (Note: after 1930 events are recorded annually)

UNITED STATES-Manners and Customs-1700-1799
                          -1800-1879
                          -1880-1900
                          -1901-1920
                          -1921-1930
                          -1931-1940
                          -1941-1960
                          -1961-

UNITED STATES-People
           -Plantation Life
           -Resources
           -Village Life
           -Western Life

UNIVERSITIES. See Colleges

VACCINATION. See Medicine; Diseases

VALENTINES

VASES. See Ceramics-Design

VEGETABLE GROWING

VEGETABLES
    Subdivided by name of vegetable and
  Collective
    See also Corn; Food-Vegetables

VENDING MACHINES

VETERANS' DAY

VIADUCTS. See Roads and Viaducts

VIGNETTES. See Design

VILLAGE LIFE. See Names of Countries-Manners and Customs;
                  U.S.-Village Life

VINES. See Plants

VIVISECTION. See Animals-In research; Biology-Zoology; Diseases;
                Medicine

WALLPAPER. See Design-Wallpaper

WATCHES. See Clocks and Watches

WATER COLOR STUDIES. See Landscapes; Marine studies; Painting-
                  Still Life; Painting-Water color

WATER SUPPLY

WAYSIDE STATIONS

WEAPONS. See Armament

WEATHER
    See also Lightning; Rain; Storms; Wind

WEATHER VANES

WEAVING. See Spinning and weaving

WEDDINGS
    See also Costume-Wedding

WEIGHTS AND MEASURES

WELLS

WESTERN LIFE. See U.S.-Western life

WHALING
See also Animals-Whale

WHARVES AND DOCKS

WHEAT

WIND

WINDMILLS

WINTER
Landscapes
-Color
Scenes
Snow Crystals

WITCHES

WOMEN IN WAR
See also Army-U.S.-Women

WOOD

WOODBLOCK PRINTING. See Design-Block printing; Engraving
Processes-Wood

WOODCARVING. See Carving

WOODCRAFT. See Boy Scouts; Girl Scouts; Handicrafts

WOOD ENGRAVING. See Engraving

WOOL

WORLD WAR I - 1914-1918

See Europe-England-History-1914-1918-European War
Europe-France-History-Third Republic-
1914-1918-European War
Europe-Germany-History-1914-1918-European War
Europe-Italy-History-1914-1918
Portraits
United States-History-1917-1921-European War
Veterans' Day

WORLD WAR II, 1939-1945
    Subdivided under theatre of operation.
  Africa
  Asia
  Europe-England
        -France
        -Germany
        -Italy
        -Russia
  European Area
  Heroes
  Naval Battles
  Officers
  Pacific Area
  Refugees
  Veterans
  Wounded

WORMS

WREATHS. See Christmas; Design-Wreath

WRECKS
  Air
  Land
  Water

WRESTLING. See Sports

WRITING
  Ancient
    Dead Sea Scrolls
    Egyptian
    Greek
    Mayan
    Mesopotamian
    Roman
  Medieval
  Oriental
  Pictograph
  Rebus

X-RAY

Y. M. C. A.

Y. W. C. A.

ZODIAC

ZOOLOGY. See Amphibians; Animals; Biology-Zoology; Birds; Coral;
Fish; Fossils; Insects; Physiology; Races; Reptiles;
Scorpions; Sea Life; Shell Fish; Shells; Snails;
Spiders; Sponges; Worms

ZOOS